I0409639

2012-2013 Presidential Election Period: National Security Considerations and Options

John Rollins
Specialist in Terrorism and National Security

October 5, 2012

Congressional Research Service

7-5700

www.crs.gov

R42773

CRS Report for Congress
Prepared for Members and Committees of Congress

Summary

A presidential election period is a unique time in America and holds the promise of opportunity, as well as a possible risk to the nation's security interests. While possible changes in Administration during U.S. involvement in national security-related activities are not unique to the 2012-2013 election period, many observers suggest that the current security environment may portend a time of increased risk to the current presidential election period. Whether the enemies of the United States choose to undertake action that may harm the nation's security interests during the 2012-2013 election period, or the existing or new President experiences a relatively peaceful period during the transition, many foreign policy and security challenges will await the Administration. Collaboration and coordination during the presidential election period between the current Administration and that of a potentially new one may have a long-lasting effect on the new President's ability to effectively safeguard U.S. interests and may affect the legacy of the outgoing President.

This report discusses historical national security-related presidential transition activities, provides a representative sampling of national security issues a new Administration may encounter, and offers considerations and options relevant to each of the five phases of the presidential election period. Each phase has distinct challenges and opportunities for the incoming Administration, the outgoing Administration, and Congress. This report is intended to provide a framework for national security considerations during the current election period and will be updated to reflect the election outcome.

Contents

Tables

Appendixes

Contacts

Introduction

Security-related implications are of concern in the lead-up to a Presidential election.[1] These concerns are present when it is known there will be a change of Administration or in cases where the sitting president is running for re-election against an opponent vying for the office.[2] A prospective presidential transition period—ranging from candidate's campaign-related activities through placement of new Administration personnel—is a unique time in American politics and holds the promise of opportunity as well as a real or perceived vulnerability[3] to the nation's security interests. On a given day the outgoing Administration has the ability to change the policies of a nation and possibly affect the international security environment, yet the following day the President and the national security leadership team may be replaced by a new set of leaders who could have very different strategy and policy goals.[4] This political dynamic, coupled with the inherent uncertainty accompanying a presidential transfer of power, may provide an opportunity for those who wish to harm U.S. security interests. Unlike other man-made incidents that may occur with little warning, the presidential election period offers a broadly defined time frame in which an enemy of the United States[5] may decide to undertake an incident of national security significance[6] to manipulate the electoral process or change the nation's foreign and domestic policies.[7]

---

[1] The Presidential election period encompasses all pre- and post-government transition-related issues and activities.

[2] While some of the risks discussed in this report are associated with a change of administration, the vulnerabilities and mitigation-related efforts noted throughout the election and transition period are applicable regardless of whether a change of administration occurs.

[3] Throughout this report, numerous references are made to the nation's increased "vulnerability" during times of presidential transition. Vulnerability is the manifestation of a potential threat to inflict harm to an area that is not properly defended, cannot be completely defended, or is indefensible. A better representation of the environment the U.S. may face during the presidential transition is the degree to which the nation is at "Risk"(R). (R) is the product of weighting and multiplying the Threat (T), Vulnerability (V), and Consequences (C) of an incident (TVC=R). (T)'s directed at the electoral process may become known by the federal intelligence community [or the federation of national intelligence activities.] The nation's (V) to a national security-related incident may be increased or decreased based on the targets chosen by enemies of the United States. (C), however, could range from minor to significant based on the severity of an incident and its proximity to the five phases of the transition period (discussed later in this paper).

[4] *The Law of Presidential Transitions*, Boston School of Law Working Paper, William P. Marshal and Jack M. Beerman, 2005. "The outgoing President retains all the formal legal powers of the presidency, yet his last electoral success is four years removed and his political capital is at low ebb. The outgoing President will want to protect his policies or accomplishments from being reversed or undermined and may also want to create obstacles to prevent his successor from too quickly achieving political and policy success. The incoming President, on the other hand, will be focused on beginning her own initiatives and may desire to expeditiously reverse the policies of the previous President." When the incoming and outgoing Presidents are from opposing political parties the conflicts during the transition period may be even more acute.

[5] Enemies that pose a risk to the United States may emanate domestically and internationally and take the form of foreign and American citizens who are aligned with philosophies, nation states, groups, or individuals that undertake action adverse to U.S. interests.

[6] While an "incident of national security significance" could entail a catastrophic natural disaster, this term, for purposes of this paper, is used to describe foreign and domestic security-related man-made acts, including a terrorist attack (in the United States, against interests overseas, or against an Ally), significant offensive action against troops deployed overseas, assassination of a U.S. or foreign leader, seizure or attacking of an embassy or consulate, a change in the political environment where the United States is undertaking stabilization activities, significant foreign power nuclear-related activity, or a foreign power or extremist group taking military action against a U.S. ally.

[7] Transitions in American government power are not reserved for the executive branch. Congressional elections and changes in state and local leadership are also occasions where individuals wishing to harm U.S. national security interests could place the nation at risk. While the focus of this paper is on security implications during a presidential (continued...)

Presidential transitions during times of global uncertainty, U.S. involvement in military operations, and risks to national security-related activities[8] are not unique to the 2012-2013 presidential election period (see **Appendix A**).[9] History shows that some state enemies purposefully select periods of government transition to undertake significant acts of violence with a desire to disrupt a peaceful transfer of power (see **Appendix B**). While the mere occasion of presidential transition does not ensure an incident of national security significance will occur, security experts argue that this window of potential opportunity is not lost on the enemies of the United States. For example, according to a 2008 presidential transition-related report provided to the Department of Homeland Security (DHS) by the Homeland Security Advisory Committee (HSAC), "briefings, research, and recent history have provided an appreciation of the potential vulnerabilities during transition periods. Not only are we [United States] aware that vulnerabilities exist, but our enemies are as well."[10] While no claims of attempting to influence the United States presidential election have been offered as a factor in the September 11, 2012, terrorist attacks on the U.S. consulate in Benghazi, Libya,[11] incidences such as this could have policy implications during the transition period.

The executive branch is not alone in attempting to ensure the country passes power from one Administration to the next in a safe and thoughtful manner.[12] However, the outgoing and incoming Administrations are viewed as primarily responsible for addressing risks to the nation and taking actions to prevent and respond to any incident that may affect the electoral process. Whether the enemies of the United States choose to undertake action that may harm national security interests during this prospective period of transition or the new President experiences a relative peaceful period shortly after entering office, many national security issues will be awaiting a new Administration. How a newly elected president recognizes and responds to these challenges will "depend heavily upon the planning and learning that takes place during the transition from one Administration to another."[13] During recent presidential transitions,[14] the

---

(...continued)

transition, it is acknowledged that planning, prevention, preparedness, response, and recovery activities could also be hampered should an incident of national security concern occur during a congressional or non-federal government election period.

[8] For purposes of this report, national security activities encompass all aspects of U.S. foreign and domestic security-related policies and operations responsible for safeguarding national security interests.

[9] For purposes of this report the presidential transition period is comprised of five phases extending from presidential campaigning activities to the newly elected President's formation of a national security team and production of accompanying strategies and policies. The five phases of the presidential transition period will be discussed later in this report.

[10] *Report of the Administration Transition Task Force*, Homeland Security Advisory Council, January, 2008. http://www.dhs.gov/xlibrary/assets/hsac_ATTF_Report.pdf.

[11] CRS Report R42743, *Recent Protests in Muslim Countries: Background and Issues for Congress*, coordinated by Christopher M. Blanchard.

[12] Other government and non-governmental entities that offer advice and assistance to presidential transition related activities include the U.S. Congress, General Services Administration, National Archives, Office of Government Ethics, Congressional Research Service, Government Accountability Office, Center for the Study of the Presidency, Council for Excellence in Government, Mandate for Leadership Project, Presidential Appointment Initiative, Reason Public Policy Institute, and the Transition to Governing Project. The United States Presidential Transition, Senate Homeland Government Affairs Committee, last accessed 14 February, 2008. http://www.senate.gov/~govt-aff/transitions/pta_page6 htm.

[13] Perils of Presidential Transition, Glenn P. Hastedt and Anthony J. Eksterowicz, *Seton Hall Journal of Diplomacy and International Relations*, Winter/Spring 2001 edition, pp 67.

[14] President Harry S. Truman is often credited with establishing the tradition of the outgoing President offering administration transition-related assistance to the incoming administration. He directed each agency leader to provide

(continued...)

---

current and incoming Administrations and Congress have traditionally undertaken numerous activities to facilitate a smooth transfer of executive branch power. Some of the actions taken during a presidential transition period include

- consulting with government and private sector experts who have presidential transition expertise,

- providing information to the President-elect after the election and prior to the inauguration,

- offering operational briefings on ongoing national security matters to prospective presidential nominees and their staff,

- preparing briefings books and policy memos detailing the issues of most concern to the current Administration, and

- expediting security clearances for president-elect transition team members.

Other activities that the current and incoming Administrations and Congress may wish to consider undertaking during the presidential transition period include

- pursuing public outreach efforts to discuss possible risks to the nation,

- involving the national security representatives of presidential candidates in all transition-related discussions,

- establishing joint advisory councils responsible for addressing all transition-related risks,

- requiring the Director of National Intelligence (DNI) to undertake efforts to support the nation's awareness of risks,

- reflecting the national security priorities of the newly elected Administration in the upcoming budget,

- passing fiscal year appropriations without undue delay,

- quickly assigning newly elected and existing Members of Congress to committees focused on national security,

- holding hearings comprised of national security experts to gather ideas on prospective U.S. national security policies and goals, and

- holding hearings soon after the inauguration of the new President to determine the Administration's national security-related priorities.

(...continued)

him a report on activities related to transitioning the new administration into power. Shortly after the election of Dwight D. Eisenhower, President Truman invited him to a meeting at the White House to discuss, among other concerns, national security-related issues. Prior to President Truman's actions and the subsequent enactment of the Presidential Transition Act of 1963, presidential transition activities rarely focused on substantive issues. The Presidential Transition Act of 1963 (P.L. 88-277) was enacted on March 7, 1964, and codified at 3 U.S.C. 102. For a more in-depth discussion of historical presidential transition processes and activities, see CRS Report RL30736, *Presidential Transitions*, by Stephanie Smith.

The Presidential Election Period

From a national security perspective, the presidential election period runs from the formal announcement of candidates for the office of the presidency to long past the inauguration,[15] members of the current Administration and potential incoming Administration may wish to initiate substantive transition activities as soon as possible.[16] Specifically, some scholars state that "enhanced cooperation and communication between the two Administrations is demanded by national security and foreign policy concerns."[17] It is further observed that, "as the world becomes more dangerous and the risks to harm more immediate, the need for effective and seamless transitions becomes correspondingly greater."[18] Thus, with respect to national security issues in particular, the need for outgoing and incoming Presidents to work together is no longer an option, but an unavoidable demand of the contemporary world.[19]

Considerations and Options that Span the Presidential Election Period

Throughout the entire presidential election period, a number of national security-related concerns and opportunities may be presented to the incoming and outgoing Administrations. However, many observers argue that the national security-related collaborative efforts of the current Administration and members of the potential new Administration, coupled with oversight activities throughout the transition period, offer the nation the best hope of being prepared to recognize and respond to acts taken to disrupt the transfer of power or change U.S. policies. In order to assess the federal governments actions related to the following issues, Congress may wish to hold classified and unclassified hearings and request reports regarding the Administration's knowledge of risks during the Presidential election period and ascertain information about the efforts by departments and agencies to ensure all applicable security and election officials are informed of potential concerns.

Possible Actions by Entities Wishing to Disrupt the Presidential Election Period

Threats during a presidential election period may be numerous with "dangers associated with the transition emanating both from within the homeland and internationally."[20] It is argued that enemies of the United States may see the nation as physically and politically vulnerable and that

---

[15] Ibid. "After the inauguration, difficult situations can also arise when a new and untested Administration faces a sudden crisis and emergency."

[16] *The Law of Presidential Transitions*, Boston School of Law Working Paper, William P. Marshal and Jack M. Beerman, 2005. "For a number of reasons there is now a greater need than any time in our Nation's history for incoming and outgoing Administrations to work cooperatively during transitions periods. To begin with, government is more complex and an incoming Administration faces an inestimable learning curve in assuming office and digesting the mounds of information necessary to be able to understand the powers at its disposal and govern effectively."

[17] Todd J. Zywicki, The Law of Presidential Transitions and the 2000 Election, 2001 B.Y.U.L. Rev. 1573 (2001).

[18] Ibid.

[19] *The Law of Presidential Transitions*, Boston School of Law Working Paper, William P. Marshal and Jack M. Beerman, 2005.

[20] Robert Landers, "*Dangers in Presidential Transitions*," Editorial Research reports, pp. 528-529.

---

disseminating threatening propaganda or undertaking an incident of national security significance during the election period could potentially result in a change in the election results or future policies. Statements or incidents may be undertaken with the desire to demonstrate a group's ability to reestablish its status as an entity to be feared,[21] intimidate the voting public, suggest perceived weaknesses in a candidate's national security experience, change the results of the election, or change future U.S. policies.

Many national security observers speculate that, if an incident of national security significance is to occur, enemies of the United States may prefer to take action just prior to the presidential election date. However, such acts at anytime during the presidential transition period could have desired and unintended effects on the presidential election and resulting policies.[22] Conversely, while many national security experts speculate that extremist groups and some foreign powers may see the presidential election period as a desirable time to undertake action against U.S. interests, the timing of such acts may be solely based on the convergence of an entity attaining a desired capability with a perceived best opportunity to successfully complete its objective.

Planning for the Unforeseen and Communicating Transition-Related Information to the Public

During previous presidential elections, some officials in the federal government have seen the need to develop options that might be pursued should the presidential election be delayed. While noting federal election dates are set by law requiring congressional action to change the current schedule, DeForest Soaries, former Chair of the United States Election Assistance Commission, wrote to then-Department of Homeland Security (DHS) Secretary Tom Ridge on June 25, 2004, that the process and procedures for changing election dates vary significantly across the nation's 8,000 voting jurisdictions. Chair Soaries suggested that the DHS and the federal interagency structure collaborate with state and local governments on a plan to address voting options, should a terrorist attack occur around the time of the election.[23] Many security experts argue that federal, state, and local election-contingency planning and coordination should occur during the early phases of the election period. It is further suggested that, in the absence of such discussions, the issuance of general guidelines, or a genuine effort toward collaboration, the prospects for

---

[21] "New Report tracks Relationship Between Al Qaeda and Jihadist Media," *CQ Homeland Security*, Matt Korade, April 4, 2008. In response to a question about Al Qaeda's troubles in maintaining support for it organization, panel members noted that the possible decline in followers coupled with the upcoming presidential election could be a potent mix for a group desperate to reassert its relevancy.

[22] For example, while the terrorist attacks of March 2004 did appear to have an affect on the election outcome and the Spanish government's support of military actions in Iraq, the new prime minister actually increased Spain's commitment to counterterrorism military efforts in Afghanistan. It is speculated that while the tactical operation may have been a success, the long-term results of the attack were counter to the strategic desires of the terrorist group. It may also be worth noting that an incident occurring during the transition period may have a relatively short-term minor effect on a targeted country based in sound principle and engendering resilient societal behavior. While the short-term affects of an attack may change the outcome of an election or a current policies, the attack may have little long-term impact on a country's societal mores and desire for a customary transfer of national power.

[23] Jim Drinkard, "United States Has No Plan for Election Delay Due to Terrorism," *USA Today*, July 12, 2004. Chair Soaries, in a subsequent interview, further stated that "each state must decide for itself what to do in the event of a disaster. When you have a national election that has serious implications, we don't have a real national standard for what constitutes a disaster. What is a disaster in Alaska may not be a disaster in Alabama. And I think this discussion on a federal level will have to also involve state officials so that we have some national consensus and can offer national guidance on what we mean by a disaster." *Countdown with Keith Olbermann*, Interview transcript, July 13, 2004.

---

electoral chaos are more likely to occur if an incident of national security significance takes place just before or on the date of election.

During all phases of the presidential transition process, many security experts suspect the federal government will receive information of concern to U.S. national security interests. Should such a heightened risk environment occur, observers suggest that one of the best ways to meet this challenge is by a showing of national unity among the outgoing Administration and individuals vying for the presidency. To support a collaborative environment, the 2008 Homeland Security Advisory Council report suggested the nominees issue a joint statement addressing potential threats to the nation or in response to an incident of national significance.[24] Some foreign policy experts suggest joint statements and activities by the current President and the prospective President-elect take place with regularity to put forth a common voice to both the American public and the enemies of the United States that security issues will be addressed in a unified and coordinated manner.

Throughout the presidential transition period the federal government may wish to undertake outreach and education efforts directed at the American public. A public awareness campaign discussing a need for citizens to be more-vigilant during the election period and providing insight into what the federal government will do in the event of an incident prior to election day may provide confidence to a concerned voting public. Activities such as this may prove useful in preparing the public for the possibility of an incident of national security significance occurring during the presidential transition period. With respect to security-related issues in the homeland, many observers argue that public awareness offers the best opportunity to provide indicators of anomalies that might be indicative of a group's preparation to undertake criminal activity to affect the presidential election process. To this degree, the DHS HSAC contends that continuous interaction with the media and the public on potential threats during this time period will improve the preparedness of the nation for an incident of national security significance. The DHS HSAC report specifically opined:

> It is important that the American public become engaged in understanding the unique vulnerabilities posed by this transition period. This will require public education and media engagement during this critical period in our history. Before, during, and after the transition, the public must learn about the choices faced by the Nation, communities, families, and individuals. The public must become a partner with their government, sharing the burden. In addition, [the] DHS should continue to engage the media as an ally in the timely dissemination of accurate and actionable information. [The] DHS must work with the multiple messengers, trusted within diverse communities, to effectively communicate this information.[25]

The DHS has the responsibility to notify the American public of current or prospective threats to U.S. domestic security interests,[26] and the Department of State has the responsibility to alert U.S.

---

[24] Report of the Administration Transition Task Force, Homeland Security Advisory Council, January, 2008. http://www.dhs.gov/xlibrary/assets/hsac_ATTF_Report.pdf.

[25] *Report of the Administration Transition Task Force*, Homeland Security Advisory Council, January, 2008. http://www.dhs.gov/xlibrary/assets/hsac_ATTF_Report.pdf.

[26] Section 203 of the Homeland Security Act of 2002 (6. U.S.C. 124), as amended by sec. 501(c)(1) of the Implementing the Recommendations of the 9/11Commission Act of 2007(P.L. 110-53, 6 U.S.C. 124), assigns the DHS Secretary with having "primary responsibility for providing warning regarding threats or risk from acts of terrorism in the homeland." However, it is common for the DHS and the FBI to make a statement or disseminate a joint bulletin regarding security issues of concern.

citizens located overseas of security-related concerns. Both organizations have numerous communication mechanisms to inform U.S. citizens and organizations regarding concerns related to the presidential transition period and, when required, to share threat information. Communication mechanisms for conveying information about the presidential transition period include the following:

- DHS: Official public announcements to the media, public service announcements, changes to the Homeland Security Advisory System, dissemination of information to state and local fusion centers and to private sector organizations, and posting information to DHS-managed websites.

- Department of State: Official public announcements to the media, warden system alerts,[27] travel alerts, country specific warnings, country background notes, and posting information to State Department managed websites.

Considerations and Options Unique to Each Phase of the Presidential Transition Period

Modern presidential transition activities are no longer constrained to the time between election day and the inauguration.[28] Some presidential historians argue that, "history tells us that any winning candidate who has not started (transition efforts) at least six months before the election will be woefully behind come the day after the election day."[29] While the time period and phases of a presidential transition are not statutorily derived, for purposes of this paper, the presidential transition period is comprised of five phases extending from presidential campaigning activities to the new President's establishment of a national security team and accompanying strategies and policies. Each phase identifies issues to consider by the outgoing and incoming Administrations and the Congress. The phases of the presidential transition are as follows:

Phase 1: Campaigning by presidential candidates.

Phase 2: Selection of party nominees.

Phase 3: Election day.

Phase 4: Post election day to prior to the inauguration.

Phase 5: Presidential inauguration to formation of the new Administration's national security team and issuance of policy directives.

---

[27] The Warden System allows Americans overseas to receive security warnings and other important notices as quickly as possible. Wardens are American citizens who will contact other Americans with relevant information from the embassy or the Department of State.

[28] "Perils of Presidential Transition", Glenn P. Hastedt and Anthony J. Eksterowicz, *Seton Hall Journal of Diplomacy and International Relations*, Winter/Spring 2001 edition. "Transition efforts in modern presidential campaigns begin well before election day."

[29] The IBM Center for The Business of Government Weblog, 2008 Presidential Transition Initiative, November 6, 2007. http://transition2008.wordpress.com/.

Phase 1: Campaigning by Presidential Candidates

Phase 1 of the presidential transition includes the time frame from campaigning by presidential hopefuls to the national political conventions that officially select the party nominee.[30] This period can last a few months to a year or longer depending on a number of factors, including the current President's desires and constitutional ability to run for re-election, the plans of individuals from the same party as that of the sitting President to challenge the President's re-election bid, and the opposing party's time frame for launching unofficial or official presidential nomination activities.

Prospective Outgoing Administration Considerations and Options

A number of activities can occur during the first phase of presidential transition activities that would benefit the incoming President and may prove useful toward providing continuity with respect to U.S. national security matters. As noted in the 2008 HSAC report, "it is important that [the] DHS take action now to ensure a seamless and agile transition to new leadership and optimize the new leadership's ability to assume operational control of the Department."[31] Recommendations offered by the Advisory Council that could be undertaken during the first phase of the transition include

- clarifying the meaning of "heightened threat" during the transition period by notifying all homeland security partners of historical patterns;

- developing contingency plans around the homeland security themes of prevent, prepare, respond, and recover;

- providing prospective presidential nominees information regarding lessons learned from incidents occurring during previous leadership transitions; and

- offering operational briefings on ongoing national security matters to prospective presidential nominees and their staff.

The current Administration may wish to consider initiating information exchanges and collaborative efforts with the opposing party candidate in this initial phase of the transition. Generally, as the campaign for President progresses through the spring and leads to the presidential conventions, relatively few candidates will emerge as viable contenders for gaining the nomination of a given political party. The current Administration could bring this relatively limited number of individuals, and their designated senior national security staff, into briefings and discussions regarding national security issues that will likely be of concern in the following year.

An issue of concern to some presidential transition observers is the turnover of personnel occupying key positions in the federal government. There are more than 7,000 federal government leadership, management, and support positions that are non-competitively filled by

---

[30] The field of presidential hopefuls may be winnowed down during this process with individuals emerging as the de facto party nominee prior to being officially acknowledged as such by the represented political party. 26 U.S.C. 9002 defines a major party as a political party whose candidate for the office of President in the preceding presidential election received 25% or more of the total number of popular votes received by all candidates for such office.

[31] *Report of the Administration Transition Task Force*, Homeland Security Advisory Council, January, 2008. http://www.dhs.gov/xlibrary/assets/hsac_ATTF_Report.pdf.

---

political appointees.[32] Some observers suggest that many of these positions have, as part of their primary function, national security responsibilities. Should large numbers of political appointees depart in the months preceding the inauguration, the federal government would likely rely on Senior Executive Service personnel, Senior Foreign Service diplomats, senior military officers, and senior general-schedule employees for continuity of operations, leadership, and management of most national security-related activities. While the occupation of senior policy positions by career government employees may not necessarily be a problem, a number of considerations arise in such an environment.

Appointing career civil servants to mid- to high-level positions in federal departments and agencies has been offered by national security observers as a way to provide continuity during presidential transitions. This action may allow agencies to operate without interruption and provide the future congressionally confirmed or presidentially appointed agency directors with in-house expertise and historical context about the organization. As a proponent of converting some of the federal government's national security leadership positions to career civil service positions, former DHS Acting Deputy Secretary Schneider noted "it's important to realize that major terrorist attacks, both here and abroad, are often launched shortly before or after national elections or inaugurations. By promoting dedicated civil servants who've proven their mettle, we're not only building for the future, but are helping ensure that during the transition, as the perceived weakness grows, our Department is prepared."[33] While the promotion of civil servants into federal agency deputy positions is welcomed by many national security observers, others are concerned with the selection process that supports this activity. Some security observers may be concerned that the individuals chosen for these positions are being selected by the current Administration's political leadership and that this may be a way for individuals with like-minded political philosophies to maintain control over an agency and pursue policies that are counter to a new Administration.

Possible Role of National Security Staff and the Homeland Security Council

The National Security Staff (NSS) is the President's principal forum for considering national security and foreign policy matters with senior national security advisors and cabinet officials, whereas as the Homeland Security Council's (HSC) purpose is to ensure coordination of all homeland security-related activities among executive departments and agencies, and to promote the effective development and implementation of all homeland security policies. The current Administration might consider temporarily establishing a joint advisory council that draws on the expertise and experience of both the NSS and HSC to assist with transition issues. This new body could be comprised of political and career staff from the NSS and HSC, outside experts with transition expertise, and members of a prospective president-elects national security team. Organizational responsibilities could include coordinating the presidential transition policies of agencies having national security missions. In assisting the transition process, the entity could attempt to ensure presidential transition period activities are coordinated in an interagency

---

[32] *Policy and Supporting Postings*, Committee on Government Reform, 108th Congress, 2nd Session, November 22, 2004. This report, popularly referred to as "The Plum Book," lists by title, type of appointment, level of position, and, if known, the name of the individual occupying the position for all non-competitive appointees who are serving during a specific administration. The report is produced during the first year of a new administration.

http://a257.g.akamaitech.net/7/257/2422/05jan20051520/www.gpoaccess.gov/plumbook/2004/2004_plum_book.pdf.

[33] "Transition: Heads We Win, Tails You Lose," *DHS Leadership Journal*, January 19, 2008. http://www.dhs.gov/journal/leadership/2008/01/transition-heads-we-win-tails-you-lose.html.

manner and are cognizant of the effects current efforts may have on a new Administration. If so desired by the President-elect, this organization could continue for a period of time into the next Administration. The council could have responsibility for advising the outgoing and incoming Presidents on possible policy implications of national security decisions made and actions taken during all phases of the presidential transition.

Office of the Director of National Intelligence

The Office of the Director of National Intelligence (ODNI) is responsible for assessing and reporting on risks to the nation and has many organizations that directly or indirectly provide analytical and operational support to the President and senior members of the national security community. The following options are activities that the DNI could undertake to facilitate the federal government's understanding and ability to respond to risks during the 2012-2013 presidential transition.

- Require the National Intelligence Council (NIC) to lead an analytic effort to assess risk to U.S. interests during the presidential transition period.[34] This effort could result in the issuance of a classified and unclassified National Intelligence Estimate discussing the intelligence aspects of the upcoming transition.

- Establish a Presidential Transition Mission Manager to lead and coordinate all federal intelligence and law enforcement analytic efforts.

- Enhance the National Counterterrorism Center's (NCTC) ability to receive and assess threat information directly related to the election period.[35]

- Ensure the DHS' Office of Intelligence and Analysis receives relevant threat information in a timely manner to facilitate sharing activities with domestic federal, state, local, tribal, and private sector organizations.[36]

- Enhance the Interagency Threat Assessment Coordination Group's ability to coordinate and report federal and local threat information that may be related to the presidential transition.[37]

- Provide the nation's state fusion centers information and specific indicators of suspicious activity that may portend possible risks associated with the presidential transition.[38]

---

[34] The NIC is a "center of strategic thinking within the US Government, reporting to the Director of National Intelligence (DNI) and providing the President and senior policymakers with analyses of foreign policy issues that have been reviewed and coordinated throughout the Intelligence Community. The work ranges from brief analyses of current issues to (strategic) estimates of broader trends at work in the world." NIC website. http://www.dni.gov/nic/NIC_home.html.

[35] The NCTC is responsible for combating the terrorist threats to the United States and managing the Nation's counterterrorism intelligence and strategic operational planning activities. NCTC website. http://www.nctc.gov/.

[36] The Office of Intelligence and Analysis is responsible for using information and intelligence from multiple sources to identify and assess current and future threats to the United States. DHS website. http://www.dhs.gov/xabout/structure/#1.

[37] The ITACG is a federal-state interagency organization with responsibility for "analyzing and assisting with the dissemination of federally coordinated homeland security, terrorism, and weapons of mass destruction information." Implementing Recommendations of the 9/11Commission Act of 2007, Sect. 210(d), P.L. 110-53.

[38] CRS Report RL34070, *Fusion Centers: Issues and Options for Congress*, by John Rollins.

Incoming Administration Considerations and Options

During phase 1 of the transition, the presidential candidates and their assembled national security teams may attempt to ascertain the current Administration's national security policies and activities and collaborate with it on issues that may affect the prospective presidency. The 2008 HSAC report proposed that the following issue areas be addressed during the transition: threats, leadership, congressional oversight, policy, operations, succession, and training.[39] While many national security observers found the report to be useful for addressing transition-related issues for the DHS, others argue that the report fell short of addressing a government-wide approach to risks and responses during the election period.[40] Specifically, some national security observers argued that the options put forth were too narrow in scope and found the report lacking in the following areas:

- Too much focus on outgoing Administration efforts, and too little attention given to the activities related to preparing the incoming Administration for the challenges it will likely face.

- Too much emphasis on the administrative process of transitioning to a new Administration, rather than ensuring incoming Administration employees are cognizant of current and projected substantive homeland security issues likely to be faced during the first year of the Presidency.

- No discussion of how state, local, tribal, and private sector leaders with homeland security responsibilities should prepare for activities related to the upcoming presidential Administration transition.

- Little detail provided on how training, education, and exercise activities can be used to prepare incoming Administration officials with national security responsibilities to be better prepared to meet current and future challenges.

Congressional Considerations and Options

Some national security observers see congressional interest in and support of presidential transitions as a crucial aspect of orderly transfers of power in the executive branch. Others argue that Congress should confine its activities to simply providing the funds necessary to support the transfer of presidential authority and act quickly to confirm the President-elect's nominated senior leadership. Regardless of the level of involvement in the presidential transition desired by the incoming and outgoing Administrations, congressional leaders may wish to pursue an active role in overseeing transition-related implementation efforts. Some suggest that without early and substantive congressional involvement in presidential transition activities foreign and domestic security risks may not be addressed in as full a manner as possible.[41]

Possible Congressional Activity. During phase 1, congressional support and inquiry may include

---

[39] While the HSAC exclusively efforts focused on assisting DHS transition efforts, many of the findings and recommendations are considered to be relevant to other organizations with national security responsibilities.

[40] It should be noted that the objective of the HSAC presidential transition report was to provide recommendations to the current DHS Secretary on matters related to homeland security. The report did not focus on issues of possible concern to the incoming Administration's nominee for Secretary.

[41] For listing of congressional legislation addressing various aspects of national security considerations during presidential transitions see **Appendix C**.

- appropriating resources to support outgoing and incoming national security collaboration efforts,

- holding classified and unclassified hearings and meetings with the both the incoming and outgoing Administrations to ascertain current transition activities,

- submitting questions to the outgoing Administration to ascertain transition planning activities and the known and projected risks during the transition period, and

- providing a sense of the Congress resolution that notes the importance of effective and collaborative activities between the departing Administration and the incoming Administration.

Congress may also wish for the current Administration to provide

- the names of agency leaders responsible for making national security-related decisions during the presidential transition period,

- briefings on the possible risks to the presidential transition process,

- information about the significant national security operations that will be ongoing during the transfer of power, and

- briefing about the Administration's efforts to engage and collaborate with prospective new Administration senior security officials.

An area of congressional interest in the past is the departure of knowledgeable political appointees and career managers during a presidential transition that may significantly hamper the federal government's ability to prevent and respond to issues of national security importance. Former Chair Thompson of the House Homeland Security Committee noted that vacancies at the DHS were "an enormous security vulnerability should an attack occur during the upcoming presidential transition."[42] Early in the presidential transition period, Congress may choose to determine the executive branch departments and agencies with national security responsibilities, review the projected leadership succession plan, and obtain the names of the individuals who have the authority to undertake action in the event an incident occurs during the transfer of power.

Phase 2: Selection of Party Nominee

Phase 2 of the presidential transition includes the time frame from the selection of individuals at the two major political party presidential nominating conventions to the day of the presidential election. This phase will last a few months as the political party conventions usually occur in the summer preceding the November election.

---

[42] "Many Vacancies at Homeland Security," *International Herald Tribune*, Brian Knowlton, July 9, 2007. In February 2008, [the] DHS provided to the House Homeland Security Committee a letter regarding departmental presidential transition related activities. The letter also contained a chart noting the occupancy status of leadership billets. Response to Chair Thompson, Congressional Quarterly Homeland Security, 14 February, 2008. In response, the DHS provided a letter to the Chair delineating senior department positions that were filled, in the process of being filled, or currently vacant.

Outgoing Administration Considerations and Options

Many national security experts suggest that phase two may be the time when the specter of increased risks to the nation is heightened. Officials at all levels of government may become concerned about national security interests being affected during the time leading up to election day. It is possible that the current Administration may consider undertaking military or law enforcement-related actions during this time to prevent a group from disrupting the election or threatening national security interests. Such actions, while possibly needed to safeguard the nation's security interest, are often the source of frustration as some question the veracity of the threat information and the need for related preventative actions. Some see these activities as pursued purely for political purposes. Others have argued that the current national security leaders are placed in an unenviable position of trying to protect national security interests during times of heightened political skepticism.[43]

With the field of potential presidential candidates likely reduced to two major party candidates, the outgoing Administration may wish to consider continuing the historical pattern of routinely providing presidential nominees and their senior staff information and briefings on matters of national security. Scholars who follow matters of national security note that, "in the pre-election period, it has proved feasible and desirable to provide intelligence briefings to candidates from both or even multiple political parties. For the most part this has been done and it should certainly be continued."[44]

Incoming Administration Considerations and Options

Section 7601 (c)(2) of the Intelligence Reform and Terrorism Prevention Act of 2004 (IRTPA (P.L. 108-458; 50 U.S.C. 435b)) allows each major party candidate for President to submit, before the date of the general election, requests for security clearances of prospective transition team members who will require access to classified information to carry out their responsibilities as a member of the President-elect's transition team. The Act further states that, to the fullest extent practicable, necessary background investigations and eligibility determinations of prospective transition team members shall be completed by the day after the date of the general election. During phase 2 of presidential transition activities, the prospective President and staff will likely undertake efforts to fully understand current U.S. national security policies and related operational activities, and may request meetings with current Administration security officials. Expedited completion of security clearance reviews for relevant personnel would greatly assist these efforts.

Congressional Considerations and Options

During phase 2 of the federal transfer of executive branch power, Congress may desire to hold hearings assessing transition-related plans,[45] and provide resources to federal and non-federal

---

[43] "Could 9/11 Haven been Prevented," *Time*, Michael Elliott, August 2, 2002. In response to a question about why the Clinton Administration did not act on information that bin Laden was most likely behind the October 12, 2000 attacks of the USS Cole (three months prior to the end of the administration), a former senior aide stated, "If we had done anything, say, two weeks before the election, we'd be accused of helping Al Gore."

[44] John Halgerson Getting to Know the President: CIA Briefings of Presidential Candidates; 1952-1992, Central Intelligence Agency, May 1996.

[45] U.S. Congress, Senate Committee on Homeland Security and Governmental Affairs, Subcommittee on Oversight of (continued...)

security entities to facilitate the transition efforts, effectuate incident deterring activities, and shore up programs that may be required to respond to an incident.

Support to Non-Federal Entities with Security Responsibilities. Some national security observers are concerned that a lack of sufficient coordination and planning between federal and state security entities could affect the presidential electoral results should an incident of national security significance occur prior to or on election day. In addition to providing funds to the prospective incoming and outgoing Administrations to support transition related activities, including national security-related support provided by departments and agencies, Congress may wish to provide resources to non-federal entities responsible for safeguarding the homeland during the presidential transition. Just as all homeland security-related incidences occur at the community level, local first responders will initially be responsible for addressing and mitigating any ongoing security concerns.[46] Whether it's a man-made incident or natural disaster, some scholars state that all levels of government may wish to consider the constitutional[47] and practical options[48] associated with a domestic security incident occurring just prior to or on the day of election.[49] Should such an incident occur, greater burden would be placed on local homeland security entities to support federal election-related activities.[50]

(...continued)

Government Management, the Federal Workforce, and the District of Columbia, *Keeping the Nation Safe Through the Presidential Transition*, 110th Cong., 2nd sess., September 18, 2008.

[46] *National Response Framework*, January, 2008. Department of Homeland Security. http://www.fema.gov/pdf/emergency/nrf/nrf-core.pdf.

[47] Some security experts are concerned about state government's ability to ensure federal elections occur in the event of an incident of national security significance. Should such an event occur on the day of the election, many options are available to allow the election to continue, including, keeping polling places open for an extended period of time or rescheduling the election on a different day. Some scholars suggest that, as "the United States Constitution explicitly delegates the authority to conduct presidential elections to the states," it can be argued that "states could create a procedure in advance that would include a provision for postponing an election, for designating particular officials to decide whether or not an election has to be postponed, and for setting out procedures for rescheduling the election." States Should Develop Procedures Now to Deal with Potential Terrorist Disruption of Presidential Election, *University of Buffalo News Release*, James Gardner, July 29, 2004.

[48] Depending on the location and nature of the incident, should a catastrophic event occur just prior to, or on election day, multi-jurisdictional decisions would be required regarding whether to reschedule the presidential election or allow for a rescheduling of the election in those localities affected by the incident. In order to abide by the Constitution and allow for the incoming administration to have time to prepare for current and national security challenges, decisions regarding the presidential election would need to be made in a relatively quick manner. The 20th Amendment of the United States Constitution states that the terms of the President and Vice President shall end at noon on the 20th day of January following an election with the terms of their successors beginning thereafter.

[49] "States Should Develop Procedures Now to Deal with Potential Terrorist Disruption of Presidential Election," *University of Buffalo News Release*, James Gardner, July 29, 2004.

[50] See generally, "Security Officials Gear Up for United States Elections," Carol Eisenberg, *Newsday*, March 8, 2008. When asked about the incoming and outgoing administration's willingness to respect and listen to each other's (national security) concerns and priorities and the effect they may have on the ability to safeguard the nation, New York State's Deputy Public Safety Secretary Michael Balboni stated, "I would love to see a seamless transition, but I don't really have much confidence that's going to be the case, given all the partisan bickering." He further went on to state that he has told his team to be prepared for anything, and that "we have to continue operating no matter what happens at the federal level."

Phase 3: Election Day

Phase 3 of the presidential transition is the day of the presidential election.[51]

Outgoing Administration Considerations and Options

Consistent with the opportunities for public outreach efforts noted in phase 2, senior federal government leaders may wish to address risks to the homeland on the day of election. In addressing any known or possible threats, senior federal officials might offer that citizen involvement in the democratic process is an effective way to demonstrate to those who wish to harm the nation that acts of intimidation will not affect the electoral process. Other actions the Administration might take to support the voting public's confidence in participating in the presidential elections include providing relevant threat information to state homeland security fusion centers in a expedited manner, working with state and local security officials to secure the nation's polling places, and increasing security for suspected targets in the United States to prevent or mitigate damage from attacks meant to disrupt the voting activities.[52]

Incoming Administration Considerations and Options

Resolving the presidential election in a timely manner is crucial to allowing the incoming Administration the time necessary to prepare for current and future national security challenges. The longer the presidential election results are delayed, the less time the current Administration has to assist the new Administration. Also, a lack of resolution could result in a delay in President-elect national security personnel appointments and possibly the U.S. being seen as increasingly vulnerable due to an uncertainty as to who will lead the country.

Congressional Considerations and Options

While the actual day of the presidential election may be uneventful, some observers argue that legislative oversight of transition activities of the current Administration taken to this point may be key to ensuring the incoming Administration is as well prepared as possible. In enacting the Presidential Transition Act of 1963, Congress provided the current Administration significant discretion in deciding the level of support to be given to the incoming Administration. In recognizing the potential risks that may be associated with a presidential transition, the Act noted the need for an orderly transfer of executive power.

> The national interest requires that such transitions in the Office of the President be accomplished so as to assure continuity in the faithful execution of the laws and in the

---

[51] Normally, the presidential election is a single-day event when the election is held with the results and determination of the President-elect to be ratified by the electoral college shortly thereafter. There are instances, such as the presidential election of 2000, where the determination of the winning candidate did not occur for approximately five weeks. As such, planning activities in support of a new administration is crucial "given that a presidential election brings wholesale change in personnel, loss of time hampers a new Administration in identifying, recruiting, clearing, and obtaining Senate confirmation of key appointees." *9/11 Commission Report*, July 22, 2004, p. 215.

[52] It should be noted that any actions taken to safeguard and preserve the sanctity of the U.S. electoral process should recognize the tension between undertaking actions in the name of national security interests and acting in a manner that could be perceived as disenfranchising certain voters, disrupting the voting process, or impinging upon individual civil liberties.

conduct of the affairs of the Federal Government, both domestic and foreign. Any disruption occasioned by the transfer of the executive power could produce results detrimental to the safety and well-being of the United States and it people. Accordingly it is the intent of Congress that appropriate actions be authorized and taken to avoid or minimize any disruption.[53]

Phase 4: Post-Election Day to Presidential Inauguration

Phase 4 of the presidential transition includes the approximately 11-week time frame from the selection of a winning candidate to the date the President-elect is sworn in to office: inauguration day.

Unique Risks to Phase 4

National security considerations unique to this phase of the transition period include incidents of national security significance that are intended to take advantage of perceived vulnerabilities attributed to an Administration that is coming to an end and a newly elected President attempting to quickly identify and designate national security personnel. Such incidents may be undertaken with the idea of attempting to have the outgoing and incoming Administrations at odds with one another with respect to presidential decision-making desires and to try and take advantage of perceived interagency coordination confusion.[54] During phase 4 many of the current Administration's political appointees resign from their positions causing some security observers to be concerned about the ability of the federal government to effectively recognize, prevent, or respond to a national security-related incident. Such a scenario may be exacerbated as the designated career civil servants that have been placed in acting capacities of political appointee positions may receive conflicting policy or operational direction from outgoing and incoming national security leaders.

Outgoing Administration Considerations and Options

While some presidential observers argue that there is little motivation for the staff of the outgoing Administration to cooperate with incoming Administration members, others suggest that, when it comes to matters of national security, the desire to protect U.S. interests and preserve the outgoing President's legacy will supersede a lack of collaboration by those soon to depart the White House. It is often observed that the level of animus shown by the outgoing President to the President-elect will have a great deal to do with the cooperation the incoming Administration's transition planning team receives from individuals currently in positions of power. It has also been noted that transitions between Administrations of the same party appear to go smoother. The President's statements and actions with respect to the ongoing transition, specifically as it involves matters of national security, will set the tone and spirit of efforts taken by current staff to

---

[53] The Presidential Transition Act of 1963, Sec. 2, March 7, 1964. 3 U.S.C. 102.

[54] Former DHS Secretary Chertoff's January 10, 2008, remarks to the DHS Homeland Security Advisory Committee: "We know that the period of transition is a period of heightened vulnerability, not because we have any specific piece of intelligence but because our observation over the last several years, including as recently as this summer when the new British Administration came in and faced attacks within a matter of days, underscores for us the fact that it is in the transition period, when people are doing the handoff, that there is a natural degree of confusion which creates an invitation to people to carry out terrorist attacks, or other damaging enterprises."

assist members of the incoming Administration.[55] Any actions or statements that are perceived to undermine the incoming Administration's policy views on national security matters could be seen as attempting to frustrate the transition process and have negative repercussions for the new Administration's efforts to conduct foreign policy or address national security-related issues.[56]

Some presidential historians see the primary role of the outgoing Administration during the post-election day period as facilitating a transparent and productive transition environment. The desire is that such actions will allow the incoming Administration to be in the best possible position to identify and respond to any significant national security issues that may arise soon after taking office. Such security-related strategic, operational, and policy transition-related activities can be offered in the form of briefings, written product, exercises to simulate day-to-day and crisis environments, and other forms of collaborative and coordinating activities.[57] Activities that could facilitate an effective national security transition include the providing of timely and relevant national security information, the formation of a transition council specifically focused on national security issues, and expediting the security clearance process for incoming members of the President-elect's national security team.

Effective Use of Presidential Transition Funds. Prior to 1963, funds were not allocated by Congress to support the presidential transition and coordination between incoming and outgoing Administrations was generally limited to the administrative issues. Since the enactment of the Presidential Transition Act of 1963, Congress has provided the General Services Administration (GSA) funds to support the substantive aspects of the incoming and outgoing change of Administration activities.[58] Historically, funds allocated for presidential transition activities have been used for travel expenses, the hiring of consultants, and reimbursing federal agencies for various types of support.[59] As authorized by the Act, funds provided by GSA to the incoming Administration can only be used from the day following the general election to 30 days after the presidential inauguration. The Presidential Transition Act of 1963, as amended by the Act of 2000,[60] authorizes the GSA to provide a greater level of support to the President-elect and prospective senior leaders of the incoming Administration. The Act allows the GSA to coordinate briefings for incoming Administration leaders, provide communication devices to these

---

[55] "The chief impediment to establishing the proper links in the past has been the fact that at the highest levels of the policy agencies virtually everyone empowered to put these support arrangements in place has been a political appointee whose loyalties are to the outgoing administration. Hence they have little at stake in supporting the incoming Administration." John Halgerson, *Getting to Know the President: CIA Briefings of Presidential Candidates: 1952-1992*, Central Intelligence Agency, May, 1996.

[56] See generally, "concerns about the volume, timing, and content of (an outgoing President's) executive orders may be heightened during presidential transition periods, particularly when the opposition party is posed to take control of the White House." CRS Report RL34722, *Presidential Transitions: Issues Involving Outgoing and Incoming Administrations*, by L. Elaine Halchin. See also, "some argue that outgoing Presidents should exercise restraint in the final months of their terms, while others would support an incumbent Administration's authority to continue to issue regulations through the end of its term." CRS Report RL34722, *Presidential Transitions: Issues Involving Outgoing and Incoming Administrations*, by L. Elaine Halchin

[57] See generally, former DHS Secretary Chertoff references providing an exit memo to the next Secretary to note homeland security-related concerns. "Homeland Security Cites Success," *United States News and World Report*, February 28, 2008.

[58] Funds authorized by Congress are only to be used to support post election presidential transition activities. All pre-election transition planning activities are privately financed.

[59] GSA, Media advisory: Presidential transition fact sheet, November 17, 2000. http://www.gsa.gov/Portal/gsa/ep/contentView.do?pageTypeId=8169&channelId=-13259&P=XI&contentId=9025&contentType=GSA_BASIC.

[60] P.L. 106-293, October 13, 2000; 114 Stat. 1035.

individuals, and create a directory of legislative and administrative materials that would be useful for new Administration leaders.

Ensure the President-Elect is Aware of Issues that May Affect National Security Interests. During this phase of the transition, every effort should be taken to apprise the incoming President and the senior national security staff of current and near-term threats that may affect United States interests.[61] While the new Administration may be aware of many strategic foreign policy and national security issues, activities relating to tactical, operational, and near-term threats will be the items most likely unknown and possibly negatively affect the new Administration soon after the inauguration. Consistent with section 7601 of IRPTA of 2004 and a recommendation contained in the 9/11 Commission report,[62] Congress requires the outgoing Administration to "prepare a detailed classified, compartmented summary by the relevant outgoing executive branch officials of specific operational threats to national security; major military or covert operations; and pending decisions on possible uses of military force." To assist with Administration national security-related transition efforts, the Act also requires the aforementioned summaries to be provided to the President-elect "as soon as possible after the date of the general elections."[63]

Establishment of a Presidential Transition National Security Coordination Council. The outgoing President may wish to consider creating a Presidential Transition Coordinating Council comprised of national security leaders from the outgoing and incoming Administrations.[64] However, unlike the formation of previous Councils, this entity would allow all members to participate in interagency discussions and decision-making activities. In assessing the concerns the incoming Administration is likely to encounter the Presidential Transition National Security Coordination Council could focus on current and short-term national security risks and applicable policy considerations.[65] A joint Administration Presidential Transition National Security Coordinating Council could

- oversee the national security transition related activities of federal departments and agencies,

- facilitate national security focused training and orientation activities to prepare incoming appointees,

---

[61] See generally, "the CIA (now the responsibility of the Office of the Director of National Intelligence) must provide support not only to the incoming President but also to his senior (national security) assistants as well." John Halgerson, *Getting to Know the President: CIA Briefings of Presidential Candidates; 1952-1992*, Central Intelligence Agency, May, 1996.

[62] *The 9/11 Commission Report*, Chapter 13.4, on effort in Congress, pp. 422.

[63] The Intelligence Reform and Terrorism Prevention Act of 2004, Section 7601, P.L. 108-458, Enacted December 17, 2004.

[64] Executive Order 13176, 5 U.S.C. 7301, Facilitation of a Presidential Transition, November 27, 2000. http://nodis3.gsfc nasa.gov/displayEO.cfm?Internal_ID=EO_13176_&search_term=13176_.

[65] In possible support for such a proposal former Homeland Security Advisor and Counterterrorism Advisor to President George W. Bush stated, "whoever the (incoming) President is has to have a national security team that can receive information and can begin to work together, literally from the time the election results are clear, through the inauguration. There's got to be a very seamless national security, homeland security transition. I've suggested that there ought to be a joint meeting between the national security officials of the current Administration and the incoming Administration and have a table-top exercise. A new Administration will have their own way of doing things, but they certainly deserve the benefit of understanding how we've gone about it during this Administration." Frances Fragos Townsend, C-SPAN interview transcript, January 4, 2008. http://www.c-span.org/special/Townsend.asp.

- discuss and collaborate on substantive national security issues that are currently underway or pending decision, and

- offer lessons learned from past policy and operational national security activities.

Expedited Security Clearance Processing for President-Elect Transition Team Members and Nominated Members of the New Administration. If not already occurring during an earlier phase of the transition period, soon after the election, it is common for the President-elect, Vice President-elect, and senior members of the incoming Administration's transition security team to start receiving classified intelligence briefings. For those individuals who do not already possess an active security clearance, the IRPTA of 2004[66] allows the President-elect to submit to the FBI or other appropriate agency the names of candidates to be nominated for high-level national security positions through the position of departmental under secretary as soon as possible after the date of the general elections. Prior to the inauguration, the FBI or other appropriate agencies are responsible for undertaking the background investigations necessary to provide appropriate security clearances to individuals who have been designated by the President-elect as key Administration officials. While the adjudication of security clearances is often a concern for individuals who have recently been hired into the federal government, it appears the FBI does have the ability to put forth the resources necessary to ensure senior national security officials are investigated and, where warranted, receive the approval to view classified material in an expeditious manner.[67]

Incoming Administration Considerations and Options

From a national security standpoint, phase 4 of the transition period is quite possibly the most hectic and exciting. With 11 weeks between election day and the inauguration ceremony, the outgoing and incoming Administrations have much work to accomplish. As the presidential transition period continues and the window for affecting the electoral process narrows, some see this phase as the most likely time for an enemy of the United States to undertake an action to attempt to throw the country into presidential decision-making chaos. With the campaigning and the election no longer a concern, the President-elect will have little time for celebration and reflecting on the past, as collaboration with the current Administration is now seen as an essential element of future success. In this regard the 2008 HSAC report proposed,

> the incoming and outgoing Administrations work closely together toward a shared commitment to ensuring a smooth transition of power. This is facilitated by a positive attitude and open mind in both incoming and outgoing Administrations, combined with the willingness to respect and listen to each other's concerns and priorities. The same attitude must also characterize the behaviors of the senior career personnel who remain with the Department and will be counted on to ensure a smooth transition between Administrations.[68]

While numerous transition-related activities commence shortly after a presidential election, some national security experts suggest that none is more important than the efforts undertaken by the national security and intelligence communities to assist in providing information and context to the incoming President and the accompanying new national security team. Given current and

---

[66] Section 7601 (f)(1).

[67] Terry Frieden, "FBI to Speed Presidential Transition Background Checks," *CNN*, November 27, 2000.

[68] *Report of the Administration Transition Task Force*, Homeland Security Advisory Council, January, 2008. http://www.dhs.gov/xlibrary/assets/hsac_ATTF_Report.pdf.

projected security challenges, "the transition can no longer be taken for granted as a honeymoon [period] and significant attention needs to be provided to managing the transition."[69] While the incoming Administration has nearly three months to prepare for assuming the presidency, many activities will need to occur in an expedited manner.[70] The President-elect will formally announce leaders of the transition team; personnel will be interviewed to possibly occupy positions in the new Administration; and interaction with the outgoing Administration, Congress, and foreign leaders may occur. The incoming Administration may also:

- Select prospective cabinet members with the desire to formally submit to Congress, for confirmation soon after the presidential inauguration (phase 5), a prioritized list of names of those individuals selected to fill key national security leadership positions.

- Select individuals to be appointed to the NSS, HSC, and others to serve as the President's and Vice-President's senior national security advisors. Generally, senior department and agency positions are left vacant until the Senate has confirmed the President's nominee. While many senior leaders of the national security community require Senate confirmation,[71] other senior political staff with significant national security responsibilities do not require Senate confirmation, including staff of the NSS and HSC.

- Create a presidential transition website to seek out individuals with national security expertise who will be needed to meet the near- and long-term challenges

- Request current Administration political appointees to remain in their jobs through the inauguration and possibly the confirmation of new national security leaders to allow for mission continuity and collaboration with new members of the Administration.[72] Overlap in key positions is allowed for limited circumstances. While agencies cannot employ multiple individuals in the same job billet ("dual incumbency"), options exist to temporarily allow both outgoing and incoming Administration personnel to be assigned to an organization.[73]

---

[69] "Perils of Presidential Transition," Glenn P. Hastedt and Anthony J. Eksterowicz, *Seton Hall Journal of Diplomacy and international Relations*, Winter/Spring 2001 edition. The authors further stated: "The United States is the sole remaining superpower, and other countries will look to it for leadership on many matters, whether the government is in a transition period or not."

[70] "Perils of Presidential Transition," Glenn P. Hastedt and Anthony J. Eksterowicz, *Seton Hall Journal of Diplomacy and International Relations*, Winter/Spring 2001 edition. The authors further stated: "The time frame of eleven weeks is simply inadequate for extensive planning in the policy or process areas. Presidential candidates need to do all they can to ensure an orderly, organized, and politically profitable transition. If Presidential candidates are successful (during the Phase for transition period), then their Presidencies can begin on a confident note. If they are unsuccessful, foreign policy (and national security) issues may overwhelm them and their presidency."

[71] Department leaders with significant national security responsibilities requiring Senate confirmation include the Secretaries and Under Secretaries of State, Defense, Energy, Justice, Treasury, and Homeland Security, the Director of National Intelligence and numerous intelligence community agency chiefs, and the FBI Director.

[72] While it is customary for the current administration's political appointees to resign prior to the new President taking office, specifically if the incoming Administration is of a different political party, "it is common for the incoming Administration to ask certain persons to remain in their jobs during the transition to ensure needed continuity during the initial period of staffing." United States Office of Personnel Management, Transition to a New Presidential Administration, OPM website. http://www.opm.gov/transition/trans20r-ch1.htm.

[73] To support national security continuity efforts and to allow incoming Administration officials to have the benefit of the knowledge and experience of their departing counterpart, OPM offers the following options: an agency can establish a different job billet to employ the designated successor for a brief period of time, OPM may authorize the use (continued...)

- Select career federal employees with significant national security expertise to be detailed to the transition team.[74] Specific focus may be given to members of the military, intelligence community, and diplomatic corps with expertise in the policy priorities of the new Administration.

- Request substantive briefings on policies and programs of interest to assess historical challenges prior to making decisions related to revising or eliminating current activities.

Some security observers are concerned about a perceived leadership void that can occur during the transition period when the outgoing Administration has constitutional authority, but diminished influence, and the President-elect has much influence, but no authority.[75] However, actions can be taken by the outgoing President and President-elect to ameliorate any suspected appearance of presidential decision-making ambiguity. For example, issues of foreign policy were hotly debated during the presidential campaign of 1992. After the general election, in which Bill Clinton was elected President, many wondered if the President-elect would attempt to initiate foreign policy changes prior to the inauguration. During the transition period, President-elect Clinton addressed these concerns by stating, "President Bush is to be viewed as the sole voice of United States policy and that the greatest mistake any adversary could make would be to doubt America's resolve during this period of transition."[76]

Also during this phase of the transition period the incoming Administration may wish to discuss prospective strategy and policy changes to national security programmatic activities with Members of Congress. If the new Administration desires to announce any new initiatives or changes to existing national security policy or programs, much work will have to be done between the time of the inauguration and the time in which the budget will need to be transmitted to Congress. After the inauguration, the new Administration will have approximately two weeks to submit to Congress a revision of the fiscal year budget proposal submitted by the previous Administration.[77]

Congressional Considerations and Options

During phase 4 of previous presidential transitions, Congress has required some agencies to have a current senior departmental official "develop a transition and succession plan to be presented to the incoming Secretary and Under Secretary for Management to guide the transition of management functions in a new Administration."[78] The deadline for submission of such a plan

---

(...continued)

of SES limited appointment authorities for short periods of time for temporary executive positions, and agencies may establish temporary transition Schedule C positions for non-executive positions to help with transitions. United States Office of Personnel Management, Transition to a New Presidential Administration, OPM website. http://www.opm.gov/transition/trans20r-ch1 htm.

[74] "Any employee of any agency of any branch of Government may be detailed to the office of either the President-elect or the Vice-President-elect on a reimbursable basis and with the consent of the lending agency head." United States Office of Personnel Management, Transition to a New Presidential Administration, OPM website. http://www.opm.gov/transition/trans20r-ch1 htm.

[75] CRS Report RL30736, *Presidential Transitions*, by Stephanie Smith.

[76] Bill Nichols, "Clinton Sets New Sights." *USA Today*, November 5, 1992, p. A1.

[77] CRS Report RS20752, *Submission of the President's Budget in Transition Years*, by Michelle D. Christensen.

[78] Implementing Recommendations of the 9/11 Commission Act of 2007, P.L. 110-53, Sec. 2405.

---

was the first of December of the year in which a presidential election occurs. While this legislative requirement appears to provide agency transition guidance that some security experts argue was lacking during prior transfers of power, others see potential problems in the manner in which it will be implemented. For an Administration's transition policy to be of strategic and substantive value, some observers recommend that the individuals responsible for drafting the plan should be career civil servants with significant experience in the agency and an expectation of remaining with the organization for the foreseeable future. This requirement would allow the main author(s) and proponent of the transition plan to remain with the agency for a prescribed period of time and provide continuity and advice to members of the new Administration.

Traditionally, Congress is out of session during much of the phase 4 transition period and may also be undergoing a change in membership. Thus congressional oversight activities during this phase are uncommon. However, some security experts contend that given contemporary risks to U.S. national security interests, a special session of Congress may be beneficial to ensuring the two Administrations are properly coordinating on national security-related issues. Once Congress returns to session and the new members are sworn in, little time is available prior to the presidential inauguration to inquire about past actions and recommend changes. A special session of Congress might be considered soon after the election to ascertain what the outgoing and incoming Administrations will do with respect to transition-related activities. If still in session during the later stages of phase 4, Congress may wish to hold hearings to assess the Administration's progress on stated national security transition-related activities. Congressional concerns during this phase might include the status of incoming and outgoing Administration collaboration efforts, how resources are being expended and toward what purpose, and to ascertain the incoming Administration's national security foreign and domestic policy goals. Congress may also wish to make itself available during phase 4 to address resource requests that emanate from the two Administrations should an incident of national security significance occur.

Phase 5: Presidential Inauguration: Placement of New Administration Officials and Formation of New Policies

Phase 5 of the presidential transition includes the time frame from the presidential inauguration to a period when the new Administration has its senior national security leaders confirmed, other non-congressionally confirmed political appointees and advisors in place, and established and implemented new national security policies. This phase can last a few months to well into the first year of the presidency.

Unique Risks to Phase 5

National security considerations unique to this phase of the transition period would include incidents of national security significance that are intended to subject the new Administration to a crisis and test the actions and policies of the new leaders.[79] An incident of national security significance could occur while the new Administration's national security leadership positions are vacant; personnel have been confirmed, but are new to their respective positions; or national

---

[79] "As recent history has shown, the most vulnerable period is 30 days prior to the election through six months after the change in Administrations." *Report of the Administration Transition Task Force*, Homeland Security Advisory Council, January, 2008. http://www.dhs.gov/xlibrary/assets/hsac_ATTF_Report.pdf.

security policies are being developed.[80] Entities that wish to affect U.S. national security interests may see this time period as uniquely vulnerable, with the President and newly assigned staff being perceived as ill-equipped to handle a domestic or foreign national security crisis.

Departed Administration Considerations and Options

While the outgoing Administration will no longer have constitutional responsibility or authority for safeguarding the country, the actions that were or were not taken prior to the presidential inauguration will be a part of the departing President's legacy. The "Protective Power" as referenced in the presidential oath "has been interpreted as investing the President with expansive authority to take actions necessary to protect the property and personnel of the United States from attack or other dangers."[81] Some scholars argue that the President's duty to protect the country is not limited to the time in which the office was occupied with responsibility extending into the next President's term to a point at which the new Administration has had reasonable opportunity to organize itself and formulate national security policies. As such, any "failure to alert and cooperate with the incoming President with respect to imminent dangers facing the nation directly exposes the country to substantial risk,"[82] and may negatively affect the previous President's legacy.

Similarly, the outgoing President should be cautious of any activity taken in the last few days of the Administration or after the inauguration that could hamper the incoming Administration's transition efforts. Such actions might include

- establishing or revising national security organizations, policies, or programs that are clearly counter to the positions of the incoming President,

- interacting with foreign leaders that may have the perception of attempting to portray future U.S. foreign policy desires,[83] and

---

[80] For example, less than five weeks after the first inauguration of President Clinton, February 26, 1993, the first attack on the World Trade Center occurred. Whether the attacks were coincidentally timed with the new presidency or the perpetrators perceived an opportunity to test the new administration is a debate among national security experts. Also, less than eight months after President George W. Bush was sworn in as the nation's forty-third President Al Qaeda launched a series of attacks on New York City and the Pentagon in Arlington, VA, with a fourth hijacked plane crashing in Shanksville, PA. At the time of the attacks, 227 of 508 (45%) of President Bush's top political positions had been filled, with 106 of the individuals in these positions on the job for less than eight weeks. Lowell Feld, "The Intelligence Community Could Not Connect the Dots, Was the Lack of Political Appointees On the Job a Reason Why?," *War Politics and Literature*, 2002.

[81] In re Neagle, 135 United States 1 (1890); Henry P. Monaghan, *The Protective Power of the Presidency*, 93 Colum. L. Rev. 1, p. 14-15 (1993).

[82] *The Law of Presidential Transitions*, Boston School of Law Working Paper, William P. Marshal and Jack M. Beerman, 2005. The authors went on further to state: "The new Administration cannot be expected to sift through complex information, much of it classified and much of it conflicting, regarding potential dangers to the United States upon taking office and still be able to craft an effective response. Reliance on the advice and direction of the previous Administration is absolutely necessary to protect the United States An outgoing President's refusal to provide that [national security-related] information and warn his successor as to potential dangers contradicts his protective duties. Accordingly, the outgoing President's decisions whether or not to brief his successor on domestic and international threats to national security are not optional. "To preserve, protect, and defend" means cooperating to the fullest degree to protect the United States against impending danger."

[83] Ibid. "The President must be aware and solicitous of the likely directions that the new President may take on foreign affairs issues and not work in a manner that may undermine the ability of the new President to achieve those goals."

- undertaking any steps that would have a negative effect or produce unintended national security consequences.

New Administration Considerations and Options

The newly elected President, who will wish to quickly set an agenda and move toward implementing goals stated during the campaign, may find the issuance of executive orders and other presidential directives as a way to distinguish new policies from the outgoing President. This may be particularly desirable when outgoing and new President are from different parties and such changes might offer the appearance of instituting a new policy direction in the early days of the Administration.[84] Likewise, the new Administration may wish to quickly promulgate national security policies and strategies for applicable departments and agencies. While the issuance of new strategies and policies may not, in and of themselves, make the country safer, they will convey the Administration's national security priorities and provide the nation an opportunity to assess the new President's intentions. In undertaking efforts to memorialize the new national security policies, many national security observers suggest that the President may be well served to proceed cautiously and take the time to review and assess current policies,[85] and listen to the views of outgoing political officials and remaining career government, military, and diplomatic personnel prior to implementing significant changes in current strategies or operations. To support continued transition efforts and to be afforded the opportunity to learn of the previous Administration's national security policy and program successes and failures, the new President may wish to have prior Administration officials maintain their security clearances and routinely receive briefings regarding current and emerging threats to United States interests.[86]

Congressional Considerations and Options

Some presidential historians suggest that legislative inquiry and support during the incoming Administration's transition efforts is crucial if Congress is to provide effective oversight during the new presidency. Professor Williams of the Massachusetts Institute of Technology argues that, "the coming transition to a new Administration and Congress opens a window for reform of the organizational structures and processes that surround planning and resource allocation for homeland (and national) security in the executive branch and Congress."[87] While the transition is an opportunity for Members and staff to interact and have substantive discussions regarding the national security policies and goals of the new Administration, some presidential historians note that "transitions are hit-and-miss affairs that handicap the new President in shifting from

---

[84] CRS Report RL34722, *Presidential Transitions: Issues Involving Outgoing and Incoming Administrations*, by L. Elaine Halchin.

[85] Regardless of the previous experience of the President and assuming best efforts are expended to support the transition by outgoing Administration officials, the new President's thoughtful decision-making efforts could encounter the challenges of a "three-part syndrome; (1) being caught by surprise by events in the domestic or foreign arena, (2) attempting to demonstrate a capacity to lead resulting in the President making hasty decisions, and (3) [perceiving] the need to demonstrate that the Administration is superior to the previous by quickly reorganizing organizations and enacting new policy." "Perils of Presidential Transition," Glenn P. Hastedt and Anthony J. Eksterowicz, *Seton Hall Journal of Diplomacy and International Relations*, Winter/Spring 2001 edition.

[86] If desired, all former Presidents and Vice Presidents are afforded the opportunity to receive classified briefings. Some suggest the new administration might benefit from other senior national security officials retaining their security clearance and being granted continued access to classified information.

[87] Cindy Williams, "Strengthening Homeland Security: Reforming Planning and Resource Allocation," *2008 Presidential Transition Series*, February, 2008 (IBM Center for the Business of Government).

campaigning to governing and create problems for the Congress."[88] Should the new Administration not make an effort to avail Congress of its foreign and domestic security policy intentions and Legislative Branch does not undertake an active role in understanding the policies and direction of the new Administration, both entities might encounter frustration as neither will feel it is receiving the necessary support to fully uphold its responsibilities. As noted by Mr. Ink, President Emeritus of the Institute of Public Administration, "new appointees are in danger of stumbling during the first crucial weeks and months of an Administration, not so much from what they are striving to do, but from how they are functioning and a lack of familiarity with the techniques that are most likely to get things done in a complex Washington environment."[89] In overseeing and supporting the new Administration's national security objectives, Congress has a number of activities it can undertake.

Prioritize Hearings for Nominated Senior Executive Branch Leaders Who Have Significant National Security Responsibilities. A congressional authority that is often noted for making it possible for the incoming Administration to be in the best position to address national security issues shortly after inauguration is to quickly confirm qualified key political appointees.[90] While Congress will also be undergoing a transition having just been sworn in two weeks prior to the presidential inauguration, some analysts see this as the ideal time for the new Congress to meet with the incoming President's national security leadership team and put in place a foundation to allow for expedited confirmation hearings soon after the President takes the oath of office. As noted by a recommendation of the 9/11 Commission Report of 2004:[91]

> Since a catastrophic attack could occur with little or no notice, the federal government should minimize as much as possible the disruption of national security policymaking during the change of Administrations by accelerating the process for national security appointments. We (9/11 Commission) think the process could be improved significantly so transitions can work more effectively and allow new officials to assume their new responsibilities as quickly as possible.

Consistent with recommendations contained in the 9/11 Commission report, the IRPTA of 2004[92] provides a sense of the Congress regarding an expedited consideration of individuals nominated by the President-elect to be confirmed by the Senate. The Act further holds that the Senate committees to which these nominations are referred and the full Senate should attempt to complete consideration of these nominations within 30 days of submission by the newly elected President. In undertaking this responsibility, many security observers see a healthy tension between Congress's desire to act quickly to hold confirmation hearings and the need to ensure that individuals with the relevant national security background and experience have been put forth by the President-elect. In many cases, highly qualified career Senior Executive Service personnel will be in an acting capacity for some of these Senate confirmed positions. Thus the

---

[88] Dwight Ink, Committee Report, Statement to the Senate Committee on Government Affairs Regarding the Presidential Transition Act of 2000, July 18, 2000.

[89] Ibid.

[90] While there is no proscriptive order in which the incoming President should nominate, or Congress should hold hearings regarding new senior Administration officials with national security responsibilities, a review of the cabinet positions noted in the Presidential Succession Act of 1947 (3 U.S.C. 19) and the previous administration's National Security Council and Homeland Security Councils may provide some assistance in prioritizing personnel placement activities.

[91] *9/11 Commission Report*, July, 2004, Chapter 13, p. 422.

[92] Section 7601(b).

perceived urgency to fill these positions quickly may be negated while Congress ensures individuals capable of meeting the demands of the position are selected and confirmed. Congress may also

- work with the new Administration to understand its national security priorities and where applicable have the changes in policies and programs reflected in the forthcoming budget;

- pass an appropriations bill without undue delay;

- quickly assign new and existing Members of Congress to committees focusing on national security issues to allow these individuals to receive briefings and understand the issues for which they have oversight;

- hold hearings comprised of national security experts and members of the new Administration to gather ideas on prospective U.S. national security policies and goals; and

- hold hearings soon after the new Administration has produced its national security strategies, policies, and presidential directives to discuss objectives and determine presidential priorities.

Conclusion

The Presidential election and transition period are characterized by unique national security challenges. In particular, if the election results in a change of Administration, a new President will likely face many national security-related challenges upon taking office. Risks during the transition period may be minimized with proactive executive branch and congressional actions. Whether the enemies of the United States choose to undertake action counter to the nation's security interests or the new President experiences a relatively peaceful period during the transition, a new Administration's recognition and response to these security-related challenges will depend heavily on the preparation and education activities that have occurred prior to the inauguration. While it may be impossible to stop an incident of national security significance during the presidential election process, there are steps that can be taken during all phases of the transition to lessen the risks to the nation. Such actions may be helpful in preparing the nation for possible risks during the presidential election period and mitigating the effects of acts taken by those that wish to cause confusion during the transfer of presidential power. The transition-related actions or inactions of the outgoing and incoming Administration may have a long-lasting affect on a new President's ability to effectively safeguard U.S. interests and may also affect the legacy of the outgoing President.

Appendix A. Recent Military Operations Occurring During U.S. Presidential Transition Periods[93]

Table A-1. Recent Military Operations Occurring During U.S. Presidential Transition Periods

Presidents	Military Operations
Carter to Reagan	In the course of a secret operation to rescue the American hostages held in Iran, a collision between a helicopter and a transport aircraft caused the deaths of eight United States servicemen on April 25, 1980.
Reagan reelection	United States forces invaded the Caribbean island of Grenada in October 1983.
Bush to Clinton	President Bush announced United States participation in the enforcement of "no-fly" zones in Iraq on September 16, 1992.
Bush to Clinton	United States armed forces were dispatched to Somalia to participate in a United States-led United Nations response to humanitarian crisis. President Bush reported the deployment to Congress on December 10, 1992.
Clinton transition	President Clinton, on January 21, 1993, stated that his Administration would continue the Bush Administration's Iraq policy.
Clinton transition	In response to an unsuccessful assassination attempt on former President Bush by Iraqi agents, the United States launched missiles targeting the Iraqi intelligence service headquarters on June 26, 1993.
Clinton reelection	President Clinton, on December 21, 1995, notified Congress that over 20,000 members of the United States armed forces would be deployed in support of the NATO forces implementing the Bosnian peace agreement.
Clinton reelection	United States armed forces were deployed in Liberia in order to evacuate United States citizens and third-country nationals who had taken refuge from the deteriorating security conditions in the United States embassy, and to defend the embassy. President Clinton notified Congress of the deployment on April 11 and May 20, 1996, noting that the deployment would continue until the security situation improved.
Clinton reelection	United States military forces were dispatched to the Central African Republic to provide enhanced security for the United States embassy in the capital, Bangui, and evacuations as necessary. The deployment was reported to Congress on May 20, 1996.
Clinton to Bush	United States military operations against Iraqi air defense forces continued in 1999 and 2000 in enforcement of the declared "no-fly" zones.
Clinton to Bush	President Clinton notified Congress on January 19, 1999, that United States forces continued to participate in the NATO-led stabilization force in Bosnia, in numbers reduced from the original deployment.
Clinton to Bush	President Clinton, on February 25, 1999, notified Congress of the continued deployment of United States military personnel in Kenya following the attack on the United States embassy there in August 1998.
Clinton to Bush	United States and NATO forces began a campaign of air strikes against Yugoslavia on March 24, 1999, in response to Yugoslavia's campaign of repression against ethnic Albanians in Kosovo. Additional United States forces provided humanitarian relief support from bases in

---

[93] Table prepared by George Mangan, Information Research Specialist, Knowledge Services Group, CRS, March 13, 2008, and updated August 30, 2012. This table is based on deployment information contained in CRS Report RL32170, *Instances of Use of United States Armed Forces Abroad, 1798-2007*, by Richard F. Grimmett.

Presidents	Military Operations
	Albania and Macedonia.
Clinton to Bush	A limited deployment of United States forces was sent to support the U.N. multinational force sent to restore peace in East Timor. President Clinton notified Congress on October 8, 1999.
Clinton to Bush	President Clinton notified Congress on October 14, 2000, of the deployment of approximately 100 armed forces personnel to provide assistance in Yemen in the wake of the terrorist attack on the *USS Cole*.
Bush reelection	Military operations against Iraq began on March 19, 2003, President Bush reported to Congress on March 21st. He notified Congress on March 20 of the continuation of a number of military operations in the war on terrorism, including actions against al-Qaeda militants in Afghanistan, cooperative operations with Pakistan in the border areas, maritime antiterrorist operations, and training in counterterrorism for other cooperating nations' armed forces. He also notified Congress on May 14, 2003 of continued United States deployment in Kosovo and adjoining countries, and on July 22nd of continued deployment in Bosnia.
Bush reelection	President Bush reported on February 25, 2004, that a combat-equipped force had been sent to Haiti to augment security forces at the United States embassy and to protect United States citizens and property. Additional forces were dispatched within two weeks, partly to make preparations for the arrival of a U.N. multinational force.
Bush to Obama	On June 13, 2008, and again on December 16, 2008, the President notified Congress, by means of consolidated reports, of ongoing U.S. military deployments and operations in support of the "war on terror" and NATO operations in Kosovo. The reports noted deployments to "locations in the Central, Pacific, European, and Southern Command areas of operation" against al-Qaida terrorists, and against al-Qaida and Taliban fighters in Afghanistan.

Note: Table prepared by George Mangan, Information Research Specialist, Knowledge Services Group, CRS, March 13, 2008, and updated August 30, 2012. This table is based on deployment information contained in CRS Report RL32170, *Instances of Use of United States Armed Forces Abroad, 1798-2007*, by Richard F. Grimmett.

Appendix B. Representative Examples of Incidents of National Security Interest Occurring During Periods of Governmental Transition[94]

This appendix provides a representative listing of incidents of terrorism that have occurred during times of transitions of heads of state. The criteria for inclusion in this chart was based on the aggressor's real or perceived intent to change the course of an election or affect future policy of the country during a time of transfer of presidential authority. It should be noted that, barring relatively few examples, there is little evidence that incidents of national security significance were planned for a specific date prior to an election. While varying levels of planning occur prior to an incident, as with most criminal acts, the leader directs, or the individuals act, when opportunity for the best possible outcome is presented. With respect to times of presidential transition, the optimal time for an attack, for a variety of reasons, may not present the best opportunity for the aggressors to attempt an incident. As such, the potential time frame for risk is present during any phase of the transition, with the effects of an incident differing based on the location of the event, the proximity to the election date, and the reaction and actions of the U.S. national security enterprise.

Many security experts believe that some of the incidences noted below had a significant impact on the outcome of the country's national election or subsequent policies. National security observers are fearful that terrorists groups may see some of the incidences as successes and feel emboldened to attempt to affect future national transfers of power by launching attack just before the election. These groups may see the timing of such an action as a viable strategic opportunity to further the goals of their cause. However, it should be noted, other security experts suggest that incidences of national significance taken prior to a national election could produce a reaction that is counter to the long-term goals of the terrorist group.

Table B-1. Terrorists Incidents that Have Occurred During Transitions of Heads of State

Type of Incident and Brief Description	Parties Involved	Date(s); Pre-election or Transition Phase
Iran Hostage Crisis "Radical students" stormed the United States embassy in Tehran and took hostage diplomats, other staff, and Marine guards. The incident did not initially appear intended to affect the upcoming United States presidential elections, but, ultimately, as the standoff lengthened, was generally agreed to have had a significant influence on the electoral contest between President Jimmy Carter and Ronald Reagan.[a]	United States, Islamic Republic of Iran.	November 4, 1979- January 20, 1981. The hostages were released as Ronald Reagan was sworn in as President.

---

[94] Table prepared by George Mangan, Information Research Specialist, Knowledge Services Group, CRS, February 28, 2008, and updated August 30 , 2012.

Type of Incident and Brief Description	Parties Involved	Date(s); Pre-election or Transition Phase
Northern Ireland, 1982 Violence in opposition to October 20, 1982, elections to form a Provincial Assembly caused more than 30 deaths by early December, including those of three Royal Ulster Constabulary policemen killed when their vehicle drove over a remote-controlled bomb.[b]	United Kingdom, Irish Republican Army, militant Protestant groups.	1982. Transition period following elections to Provincial Assembly.
Bombing of Marine Barracks, Beirut, Lebanon A truck bomb destroyed the compound housing United States Marines near Beirut airport, killing 242 Americans. Islamic Jihad claimed responsibility for the attack. The Reagan Administration's Lebanon policy quickly became a campaign issue due to questions raised by Democratic presidential candidates.[c]	United States, Islamic Jihad.	October 23, 1983. Pre-election.
Bioterrorism in the United States Disciples of Bhagwan Shree Rajneesh deliberately contaminated salad bars in ten restaurants with salmonella, causing over 700 people to become ill. The plot was designed to put out of action enough voters so that Rajneesh's followers could swamp the polls and elect an all-Rajneeshi slate of candidates, thereby taking over the county government, with which the Rajneeshis had disputes.[d]	Wasco County, Oregon, followers of Bhagwan Shree Rajneesh.	September 9, 1984. Pre-election.
Assassination of President of Lebanon President Rene Moawad was killed when a remote-controlled bomb detonated as his car passed over it. Twenty-three other persons were also killed.[e] He had held office for only 17 days.	Government of Lebanon, unknown parties.	November 22, 1989. Transition period.
Assassination of Rajiv Gandhi Former Indian Prime Minister Rajiv Gandhi, campaigning for his Congress Party in national elections, was killed, along with 14 others, when a female suicide bomber detonated herself next to him at a campaign appearance.[f]	Congress Party (India), Liberation Tigers of Tamil Eelam (LTTE).	May 22, 1991. During national voting period.
IRA Attacks in Britain The Irish Republican Army conducted a bombing campaign in Britain explicitly aimed at influencing the upcoming general election: "These attacks signal our determination and resolve to focus the government's attention on their war in Ireland. As they face into a general election, our volunteers will continue to force their occupation of part of our country onto the British political agenda."[g]	United Kingdom, Irish Republican Army.	March 1992. Pre-election.
Omagh Bombing, Northern Ireland, 1998 News reports cite speculation that a bomb attack that killed at least 28 people and wounded over 200 was carried out by the I.R.A. splinter group "Real I.R.A." in an attempt to wreck the peace agreement overwhelmingly approved by referendum in both Northern Ireland and the Irish Republic.[h]	United Kingdom, "Real I.R.A."	August 15, 1998. Post-referendum transition period.

Type of Incident and Brief Description	Parties Involved	Date(s); Pre-election or Transition Phase
Russian Apartment Building Explosions Massive explosions caused heavy casualties in nighttime attacks on apartment buildings, one in Dagestan, two in Moscow, and another in Volgodonsk. The four blasts over a 16 day period killed approximately 300 people.[i] Government officials blamed Islamic extremists for the attacks, which occurred in the last year of Boris Yeltsin's presidency, shortly after the appointment of Vladimir Putin as Prime Minister.	Russia, Islamic extremists from the Caucasus area (as stated by Russian authorities).	September 1999. Transitional period leading up to presidential election.
Assassination of State Assembly Member, Threats Against Elections A Pakistan-based group claimed responsibility for the assassination of a member of the new Jammu and Kashmir Assembly, Abdul Aziz Mir. During the elections for the Assembly, which were held the previous fall, the group had threatened to kill anyone participating in the campaign.[j]	India, Save Kashmir Movement.	December 20, 2002. Pre-election and transition period.
Suicide Bombing of Commuter Train, Russia A suicide bomber detonated over 20 pounds of explosives aboard a commuter train in the Stavropol region (near Chechnya). Forty-seven persons were killed and 155 injured, many seriously. The attack took place two days before national elections.[k]	Russia, unknown parties (Chechen independence leader Aslan Maskhadov denied responsibility).	December 5, 2003. Pre-election.
Bombings of Commuter Trains, Madrid, Spain Ten backpack bombs set off in crowded commuter trains killed 191 people and injured nearly 2,000. Although the government claimed that the Basque separatist group ETA was responsible, many Spaniards believed that the attack was in retaliation for their government's support of the United States' actions in Iraq, and voted into office the Socialist Workers' Party, whose leader, Jose Luis Rodriguez Zapatero, had promised to withdraw all 1,300 Spanish troops from Iraq.[l]	Spain, al-Qaeda affiliates.	March 11, 2004. Pre-election.
Attempted Bombings of London Nightclub District and Glasgow Airport Two men believed to be hardline Islamists carried out two bombing attempts early in the transition period between the governments of Prime Ministers Tony Blair and Gordon Brown. The first was the attempted bombing of an area of nightclubs in London's West End, using fuel bomb devices placed in two Mercedes Benz automobiles. The terrorists' remote detonation attempts failed and the bombs were disarmed. In the second incident, the attackers rammed a blazing Jeep Cherokee loaded with extra fuel into the terminal at Glasgow airport. The driver, Kafeel Ahmed, an engineer, later died of burns in hospital. The passenger, identified as Dr. Bilal Abdulla, a British National Health Service physician, was not seriously injured.[m]	United Kingdom, radical Islamists, possibly Al Qaeda sympathizers.	June 29-30, 2007. Governmental transition period.

Type of Incident and Brief Description	Parties Involved	Date(s); Pre-election or Transition Phase
Assassination of Former Prime Minister, Pakistan Former Pakistani Prime Minister Benazir Bhutto, campaigning for parliamentary elections to be held January 8, 2008, was killed along with over 20 other persons in an attack attributed to militant Islamists. A suicide bomber, possibly accompanied by an accomplice firing pistol shots, detonated next to her car following a political rally. Various reports assigned responsibility for the assassination to Al Qaeda's second-in-command, Ayman Al-Zawahiri, or to Baitullah Mehsud, a top Taliban commander in the South Waziristan region of Pakistan. The elections were postponed.[n]	Pakistan, Islamist militants.	December 27, 2007. Pre-election.
Murder of Former Local Government Official, Spain A former city council member in northern Spain was shot to death in front of his wife and child by a suspected ETA gunman. The principal Spanish political parties condemned the attack and suspended campaigning for national elections due to be held two days later.[o]	Spain, ETA.	March 7, 2008. Pre-election.
Coordinated Bombings At Five Sites In Indian Capital Kill 18 A synchronized series of explosions caused mass casualties at crowded locations in New Delhi during the lead-up to national elections, in which the nation's response to terrorism had become a major issue. A group calling itself "Indian Mujahedeen" had emailed a warning of attacks to television stations earlier in the evening.[p]	India, Indian Mujahedeen.	September 13, 2008. Pre-election.
Intimidation Attacks Against Party Officials in Indonesia Various forms of violence, including grenade assaults and shootings, were employed during the months prior to national parliamentary elections against officials of the Aceh Party, the political party of the Free Aceh Movement, which signed a peace treaty with the Indonesian government in 2005 after nearly three decades of armed struggle. Five Aceh Party officials were shot to death in the attacks.[q]	Aceh Party, unknown assailants [suspected to be Indonesian military or military-backed].	Elections held April 9, 2009. Pre-election.
Insurgent Attacks Against Political and Electoral Targets In Afghanistan In the weeks prior to August 20 national elections, Afghanistan saw a sharp surge in bombings, shootings, and rocket attacks committed by militants against campaign workers, electoral sites, and government officials. Taliban fighters threatened retaliation against voters, and according to news reports many potential voters stayed away from the polls because of the potential for violence.[r]	Afghanistan, Taliban insurgents.	Elections held August 20, 2009. Pre-election.
Destabilization Attacks Against Iraqi Government Prior to Elections A campaign of attacks against government targets prior	Iraq; Iraqi insurgents [Prime Minister Maliki attributed attacks to the group al-Qaeda In	Elections originally scheduled for January 16, 2010, postponed until March 7 due to political

Type of Incident and Brief Description	Parties Involved	Date(s); Pre-election or Transition Phase
to January 16 national parliamentary elections culminated in a massive, coordinated suicide truck bomb assault against the Iraqi Justice Ministry and provincial council complexes in a highly-secured area of Baghdad. At least 132 were killed and over 520 wounded, according to published reports. Subsequent attacks involving remotely-detonated and suicide bombs killed hundreds more after the elections were postponed until March due to unresolved ethnic and sectarian disputes.[s]	Mesopotamia and Baath Party remnants].	infighting. Pre-election.
Mass Kidnapping and Murders Linked to Philippine Elections Over 40 persons were kidnapped and at least 21 later found dead in one incident of election-related violence occurring after a group of a candidate's supporters attempted to file candidacy papers for him at an electoral office. According to a news report, an Islamist insurgency and clan wars raise the potential for electoral violence in the province in which the incident occurred.[t]	Candidate's supporters, unknown persons	November 23, 2009. Pre-election.
Taliban Attacks Affect Voter Turnout in Afghan Parliamentary Elections Taliban insurgents employed small-arms fire, rocket attacks, and bombings in a concerted effort to drive potential voters away from the polls during national parliamentary elections.[u]	Afghanistan, Taliban insurgents	September 18, 2010. Pre-election.

a. Mickolus, Edward F., *Transnational Terrorism: A Chronology of Events, 1968-1979*, Westport, Connecticut, Greenwood Press, 1980, as updated in subsequent editions. During the Presidency of Jimmy Carter, Iranian militants stormed the United States Embassy and took 66 Americans captive. While many national security experts suggest the taking of hostages in the United States Embassy in Iran in November 1979 was in response to United States policies, it does not appear that this activity was a direct attempt to affect the United States presidential election of 1980. However, many national security observers suggest the hostage taking actions by the Iranian militants, coupled with the duration that the hostages remained in captivity (444 days) and the United States military's failed rescue attempt in April of 1980, was a contributing factor to President Carter not being reelected. On January 20, 1981, Ronald Reagan was inaugurated President and the hostages were released later that day.

b. "A Vicious Tribalism' Alarms Ulster," *New York Times*, October 31, 1982; "Flight Of Talent Called Peril To Ulster's Future," *New York Times*, December 13, 1982.

c. "Democrats Expect To Campaign On Lebanon Issue," *New York Times*, October 25, 1983.

d. Source: Praeger Security International's Terrorism, Homeland Security, Strategy database.

e. "Lebanese Lawmakers Meet To Plan Election Of Slain President's Successor," *New York Times*, November 24, 1989, p. A3.

f. Mickolus, Edward F., *Terrorism, 1988-1991*, Westport, Connecticut, Greenwood Press, 1993.

g. "I.R.A. Is Vowing Further Attacks In Effort To Disrupt British Election," *New York Times*, March 2, 1992.

h. "The Day After In Ulster Town: Now 'It's Back,'" *New York Times*, August 17, 1998, p. A1.

i. "Russia's War Hits Home," *Newsweek*, September 27, 1999.

j. Source: Praeger Security International's Terrorism, Homeland Security, Strategy database.

k. Source: Praeger Security International's Terrorism, Homeland Security, Strategy database.

l. Source: Praeger Security International's Terrorism, Homeland Security, Strategy database.

m. "Britain Under Attack As Bombers Strike At Airport," July 1, 2007; "Five Under Guard As Police Link London and Glasgow Attacks, July 2, 2007; "Airport Bomb Suspects 'Left Behind Suicide Note Detailing Their Motives,'" July 5, 2007; all from *The Times* (London).

n. Source: Terrorism Knowledge Base, Memorial Institute for the Prevention of Terrorism http://www.tkb.org.

o. "Killing In Spain Curtails Campaign," *New York Times*, March 8, 2008.

p. "Explosions at 5 Sites in India's Capital Kill 18," *New York Times*, September 14, 2008.

q. "Democracy in Indonesia: The Next Test," *New York Times*, April 9, 2009.

r. "A Top Leader of the Taliban Is Captured At a Clinic," *New York Times*, August 28, 2009; "Wide Fraud Is Charged As Afghans Tally Votes," *New York Times*, August 26, 2009; "Violence Hits Afghanistan Just Two Days Before Voting," *New York Times*, August 19, 2009; "Taliban Threats May Sway Vote In Afghanistan," *New York Times*, August 17, 2009.

s. "Deadliest Bombs Since '07 Shatter Iraqi Complexes," *New York Times*, October 26, 2009; "For Every Iraqi Party, an Army of Its Own," *New York Times*, October 29, 2009; "Iraqis Defy Blasts in Strong Turnout for Pivotal Vote," *New York Times*, March 8, 2010.

t. "21 Reported Dead and 22 Missing in Mass Kidnapping Tied to Philippine Election," *New York Times*, November 24, 2009.

u. "Light Turnout in Afghan Parliamentary Elections as Violence Deters Voters," *New York Times*, September 19, 2010.

Appendix C. Congressional Legislation Addressing Various Aspects of National Security Considerations During Presidential Transitions, in Chronological Order (1963-2008)

Table C-1. Congressional Legislation Addressing Various Aspects of National Security Considerations During Presidential Transitions, in Chronological Order (1963-2008)

Congress and Session Introduced	Date Introduced	Bill	Title	Public Law (date became law)	Time Since Last Transition[a]	Time Until Next Scheduled Transition[a]
111th, 2nd Session	April 13, 2010	S. 3196	Pre-Election Presidential Transition Act of 2010	P.L. 111-283 (Oct. 15, 2010)	1 year, 3 months	2 years, 9 months
111th, 2nd Session	December 17, 2010	H.R. 6557	Presidential Succession Act of 2010		1 year, 11 months	2 years, 1 month
110th, 1st Session	January 17, 2007	H.R. 540	Presidential Succession Act of 2007		6 years	2 years
109th, 1st Session	April 27, 2005	S. 920	Presidential Succession Act of 2005		4 years, 3 months	3 years, 9 months
109th, 1st Session	April 27, 2005	H.R. 1943	Presidential Succession Act of 2005		4 years, 3 months	3 years, 9 months
108th, 2nd Session	Sept. 7, 2004	S. 2774	9/11 Commission Report Implementation Act of 2004		3 years, 8 months	4 months
108th, 2nd Session	Sept. 8, 2004	H.R. 5024	9/11 Commission Recommendations Implementation Act of 2004		3 years, 8 months	4 months
108th, 2nd Session	Sept. 9, 2004	H.R. 5040	9/11 Commission Report Implementation Act of 2004		3 years, 8 months	4 months
108th, 2nd Session	Sept. 14, 2004	H.Res. 775	Expressing the sense of the House of Representatives with respect to the continuity of Government and the smooth transition of executive power		3 years, 8 months	4 months
108th, 2nd Session	Sept. 23, 2004	S. 2845	Intelligence Reform and Terrorism Prevention Act of 2004	P.L. 108-458 (Dec. 17, 2004)	3 years, 8 months	4 months
108th, 2nd Session	Sept. 24, 2004	H.R. 10	9/11 Recommendations Implementation Act		3 years, 8 months	4 months
108th, 2nd Session	Oct. 5, 2004	H.R. 5223	National Intelligence Reform Act of 2004		3 years, 9 months	3 months
88th, 1st Session	Apr. 24, 1963	H.R. 4638	Presidential Transition Act of 1963	P.L. 88-277 (Mar. 7, 1964)	2 years, 3 months	1 year, 9 months

Note: Prepared by Ryan Granger, Information Research Specialist, Knowledge Services Group, CRS, February 28, 2008; updated by George Mangan, Information Research Specialist, Knowledge Services Group, CRS, September 4, 2012.

a.   As of date introduced.

Author Contact Information

John Rollins
Specialist in Terrorism and National Security
jrollins@crs.loc.gov, 7-5529

www.ingramcontent.com/pod-product-compliance
Lightning Source LLC
Chambersburg PA
CBHW080631290526
45790CB00007B/3018